Nonia Books

Published in 2024 by Nonia Books
Copyright © 2024 by Avinash Prasad

100 Life Changing Quotes
ISBN: 978-93-340-2239-1

Your vision will become clear
only when you can look into
your own heart.
Who looks outside, dreams;
who looks inside, awakes.

Carl Jung

 # 1

Don't ask what the world needs.
Ask what makes you come alive
and go do it. Because what the
world needs is people who have
come alive.

Howard Thurman

2

Your solitude will be a support and a home for you, even in the midst of very unfamiliar circumstances, and from it, you will find all your paths.

Rainer Maria Rilke

 # 3

I think it's very healthy to spend time alone. You need to know how to be alone and not be defined by another person.

Oscar Wilde

\# 4

The purpose of our lives is to be happy. If you want to be happy, practice compassion. The ultimate source of happiness is warm-heartedness.

Dalai Lama

5

To live a creative life, we must lose our fear of being wrong. The only true wisdom is in knowing you know nothing.

Socrates

6

When everything seems to be going against you, remember that the airplane takes off against the wind, not with it.

Henry Ford

Loyalty is not passive. It's active. It's not something you should just feel. It's something you should demonstrate.

Adam Grant

8

The true test of character is not how much we know how to do, but how we behave when we don't know what to do.

John W. Holt Jr.

9

When you have made your choice, it is providence that is your guide. Good, bad, or indifferent. Your fate lies in that.

Morgan Freeman

10

You can design and create, and build the most wonderful place in the world. But it takes people to make the dream a reality.

Walt Disney

11

"

Live life as though nobody is watching, and express yourself as though everyone is listening.

Nelson Mandela

12

Keep away from those who try to belittle your ambitions. Small people always do that, but the really great make you believe that you too can become great.

Mark Twain

13

Always be yourself, express yourself, have faith in yourself, do not go out and look for a successful personality and duplicate it.

Bruce Lee

14

Most people work just hard enough not to get fired and get paid just enough money not to quit.

George Carlin

15

When you are asked if you can do a job, tell 'em, 'Certainly I can! ' Then get busy and find out how to do it.

Theodore Roosevelt

16

In the end, just three things matter: How well we have lived. How well we have loved. How well we have learned to let go.

Jack Kornfield

17

Good health is not something we can buy. However, it can be an extremely valuable savings account.

Anne Wilson Schaef

18

Humility is the key to true greatness. The more we come to recognize our own insignificance, the more we mature into authentic greatness.

Craig D. Lounsbrough

19

The greater danger for most
of us lies not in setting our
aim too high and falling short,
but in setting our aim too low
and achieving our mark.

Michelangelo

20

Anger is like a storm rising up from the bottom of your consciousness. When you feel it coming, turn your focus to your breath.

Thich Nhat Hanh

 # 21

You are responsible for your life. You can't keep blaming somebody else for your dysfunction. Life is really about moving on.

Oprah Winfrey

 # 22

Do the difficult things while they are easy and do the great things while they are small. A journey of a thousand miles must begin with a single step.

Lao Tzu

23

It is not the strongest of the species that survive, nor the most intelligent, but the one most responsive to change.

Mahatma Gandhi

24

It is not the strongest of the species that survive, nor the most intelligent, but the one most responsive to change.

Charles Darwin

You never change things by fighting the existing reality. To change something, build a new model that makes the existing model obsolete.

Buckminster Fuller

26

It's so hard to forget pain, but it's even harder to remember sweetness. We have no scar to show for happiness. We learn so little from peace.

Chuck Palahniuk

The hardest thing you can do
is smile when you are ill, in
pain, or depressed. But this
no-cost remedy is a necessary
first half-step if you are to
start on the road to recovery.

____

Allen Klein

 # 28

Sometimes it takes a
heartbreak to shake us awake
and help us see we are
worth so much more than
we're settling for.

Mandy Hale

29

We shall not cease from exploration, and the end of all our exploring will be to arrive where we started and know the place for the first time.

T. S. Eliot

 # 30

It's not about perfect. It's about effort. And when you bring that effort every single day, that's where transformation happens. That's how change occurs.

Jillian Michaels

31

Imperfection is beauty, madness is genius, and it's better to be absolutely ridiculous than absolutely boring.

Marilyn Monroe

 # 32

Do not go where the path may lead, go instead where there is no path and leave a trail. Life is a journey that must be traveled no matter how bad the roads and accommodations.

Ralph Waldo Emerson

 # 33

If you love somebody, let
them go, for if they return,
they were always yours. And
if they don't, they never were.

Khalil Gibran

34

The only limit to our realization of tomorrow will be our doubts of today. The greatest glory in living lies not in never falling, but in rising every time we fall.

Rabindranath Tagore

 # 35

Building life is not just about creating a structure, but also about weaving experiences, emotions, and memories into its foundation.

Avinash Prasad

 # 36

The two most powerful warriors are patience and time. The strongest of all warriors are these two—Time and Patience.

Leo Tolstoy

It is not the failure of others to
appreciate your abilities
that should trouble you,
but rather your failure to
appreciate theirs.

Confucius

 # 38

You have power over your
mind - not outside events.
Realize this, and you will
find strength.

Marcus Aurelius

Reshape yourself through the power of your will; never let yourself be degraded by self-will. The will is the only friend of the self, and the will is the only enemy of the self.

**Bhagavad Gita 6.5
(Mahabharata)**

40

If you want to know what a
man's like, take a good look at
how he treats his inferiors,
not his equals.

J. K. Rowling

41

66

Our life is shaped by our mind; we become what we think. Joy follows a pure thought like a shadow that never leaves.

Gautama Buddha

42

We cannot choose our external circumstances, but we can always choose how we respond to them.

Epictetus

43

66

Many of life's failures are
people who did not realize
how close they were to
success when they gave up.

Thomas A. Edison

44

Talk to yourself once in a day, otherwise you may miss meeting an intelligent person in this world.

Swami Vivekananda

45

The truth is always an abyss.
One must — as in a swimming
pool — dare to dive from the
quivering springboard of trivial
everyday experience and sink
into the depths.

Franz Kafka

46

Learn from yesterday, live for today, hope for tomorrow. The important thing is not to stop questioning.

____

Albert Einstein

47

A sense of humor... is needed armor. Joy in one's heart and some laughter on one's lips is a sign that the person down deep has a pretty good grasp of life.

Hugh Sidey

48

Let your plans be dark and
impenetrable as night,
and when you move, fall like
a thunderbolt.

Sun Tzu

49

>

Your task is not to seek for love,
but merely to seek and find all
the barriers within yourself that
you have built against it.

———————————————

Rumi

 # 50

If you want to be creative, stay in part a child, with the creativity and invention that characterizes children before they are deformed by adult society.

Jean Piaget

The truth is, everyone is going
to hurt you.
You just got to find the ones
worth suffering for.

Bob Marley

 # 52

You miss 100% of the shots you don't take. Life is 10% what happens to us and 90% how we react to it.

Wayne Gretzky

 # 53

> Be not afraid of greatness: some are born great, some achieve greatness, and some have greatness thrust upon them.

William Shakespeare

54

The only rule is don't be
boring and dress cute
wherever you go.
Life is too short to blend in.

____

Paris Hilton

55

Remember to look up at the
stars and not down at your feet.
Try to make sense of what you
see and wonder about what
makes the universe exist.
Be curious.

Stephen Hawking

 # 56

> Wise leaders generally have wise counselors because it takes a wise person themselves to distinguish them.

Diogenes of Sinope

57

Character is like a tree and reputation like a shadow. The shadow is what we think of it; the tree is the real thing.

Abraham Lincoln

 # 58

We are not human beings having a spiritual experience. We are spiritual beings having a human experience.

Pierre Teilhard de Chardin

 # 59

The only thing standing
between you and your goal is
the story you keep telling
yourself as to why you can't
achieve it.

Jordan Belfort

 # 60

We all want to help one another.
Human beings are like that.
We want to live by each
other's happiness, not by each
other's misery.

Charlie Chaplin

61

> Life is not measured by the
> breaths we take,
> but by the moments that take
> our breath away.

Cleopatra

62

Morality is not the doctrine of how we may make ourselves happy, but how we may make ourselves worthy of happiness.

Immanuel Kant

 # 63

Champions aren't made in the gyms. Champions are made from something they have deep inside them—a desire, a dream, a vision.

Muhammad Ali

64

Credit buying is much like being
drunk. The buzz happens
immediately, and it
gives you a lift. The hangover
comes the day after.

____

Joyce Brothers

65

Death is not the greatest loss in life. The greatest loss is what dies inside while still alive. Never surrender.

Tupac Shakur

 # 66

> The difference between a successful person and others is not a lack of strength, not a lack of knowledge, but rather a lack in will.

Vince Lombardi

Don't take rest after your first victory because if you fail in the second, more lips are waiting to say that your first victory was just luck.

A. P. J. Abdul Kalam

68

You can't connect the dots looking forward; you can only connect them looking backward. So you have to trust that the dots will somehow connect in your future.

Steve Jobs

69

Non-violence is not inaction.
It is not discussion.
It is not for the timid or weak.
Non-violence is hard work.

Cesar Chavez

 # 70

Maturity is the ability to think,
speak and act your
feelings within the bounds
of dignity.

Samuel Ullman

71

The willingness to accept responsibility for one's own life is the source from which self-respect springs.

Joan Didion

72

Optimism is the faith that
leads to achievement.
Nothing can be done without
hope and confidence.

Helen Keller

> You have not lived today
> until you have done
> something for someone who
> can never repay you.

John Bunyan

74

Remember there's no such thing as a small act of kindness. Every act creates a ripple with no logical end.

Scott Adams

75

We are more often frightened
than hurt,
and we suffer more from
imagination than from reality.

Seneca

76

The most truly generous
persons are those who
give silently without hope of
praise or reward.

____

Carol Ryrie Brink

 # 77

Patience serves as a protection against wrongs as clothes do against cold.
For if you put on more clothes as the cold increases, it will have no power to hurt you.

Leonardo da Vinci

 # 78

Fashion is about dressing
according to what's fashionable.
Style is more about
being yourself.

Oscar de la Renta

79

The hardest challenge is to be yourself in a world where everyone is trying to make you be somebody else.

E. E. Cummings

80

Many ideas grow better when transplanted into another mind than the one where they sprang up.

Oliver Wendell Holmes

81

Anybody can become angry – that is easy, but to be angry with the right person and to the right degree and at the right time and for the right purpose, and in the right way – that is not within everybody's power and is not easy.

Aristotle

82

A sense of humor is part of
the art of leadership, of getting
along with people, of getting
things done.

Dwight D. Eisenhower

 # 83

Within you, there is a stillness
and a sanctuary to which
you can retreat at any time and
be yourself.

Hermann Hesse

84

The spirit, the will to win, and the will to excel are the things that endure. These qualities are so much more important than the events that occur.

Vince Lombardi

 # 85

The only way to deal with fear is to face it. You can't deny it, you can't ignore it. The spirit of fear is real, but you have to find the courage to stare it down.

T. D. Jakes

 # 86

Scars are like battle wounds - beautiful, in a way. They show what you've been through and how strong you are for coming out of it.

Demi Lovato

The press is the best instrument for enlightening the mind of man, and improving him as a rational, moral, and social being.

Thomas Jefferson

 # 88

> Power is given only to those who dare to lower themselves and pick it up. Only one thing matters, one thing: to be able to dare!

Fyodor Dostoevsky

89

"

True silence is the rest of the mind, and is to the spirit what sleep is to the body, nourishment and refreshment.

William Penn

90

Peace is the result of retraining your mind to process life as it is, rather than as you think it should be.

Wayne W. Dyer

91

History, despite its wrenching pain, cannot be unlived, but if faced with courage, need not be lived again.

Maya Angelou

92

Never forget what you are, for surely the world will not. Make it your strength. Then, it can never be your weakness. Armour yourself in it, and it will never be used to hurt you.

George R. R. Martin

93

Be alone,
that is the secret of invention;
be alone,
that is when ideas are born.

Nikola Tesla

94

Your work is going to fill a large part of your life, and the only way to be truly satisfied is to do what you believe is great work. And the only way to do great work is to love what you do.

Steve Jobs

95

History is a relentless master. It has no present, only the past rushing into the future. To try to hold fast is to be swept aside.

John F. Kennedy

96

The food you eat can be either the safest and most powerful form of medicine or the slowest form of poison.

Ann Wigmore

97

Community is a sign that love is possible in a materialistic world where people so often either ignore or fight each other. It is a sign that we don't need a lot of money to be happy-in fact, the opposite.

Jean Vanier

98

Ideas are like rabbits. You get a couple and learn how to handle them, and pretty soon you have a dozen.

John Steinbeck

99

Don't compare yourself
with anyone in this world.
If you do so, you are
insulting yourself.

Bill Gates

100